A Letter From Tamar

Finding Victory Over Sexual Abuse and Preventing the Cycle in Your Family

M. Ojinga & Dionne Harrison MD

WestBow Press books may be ordered through booksellers or by contacting:

WestBow Press
A Division of Thomas Nelson & Zondervan
1663 Liberty Drive
Bloomington, IN 47403
www.westbowpress.com
844-714-3454

ISBN: 978-1-4908-0594-8 (sc)
ISBN: 978-1-4908-0595-5 (e)

Library of Congress Control Number: 2013917615

Print information available on the last page.

WestBow Press rev. date: 07/12/2023

WESTBOW
PRESS®
A DIVISION OF THOMAS NELSON
& ZONDERVAN

Introduction

This book aims to increase families' awareness about sexual abuse and teach children to "tell it" if it occurs. Tamar's story is re-told in 2 parts: the first is a prevention narrative emphasizing truth telling; the second half is specifically for families and counselors/therapists to help children who have experienced sexual abuse. Care has been taken to avoid "too much" information for young readers (7 years &older). We believe it is best for parents and counselors to decide what detail about sexual abuse is necessary and appropriate for each child. First, read the online Discussion Guide at ALetterFromTamar.com. Next, review A Letter From Tamar. Then, browse the online Discussion Cards for suggested concepts to emphasize while reading the book to your child. Finally, read the story to your child/ren.

A Letter from Tamar is only part of a total care plan for victory over sexual abuse. Reporting sexual offenders can bring about much conflict, but is a necessary step in rebuilding trust and a sense of safety for the child. This sexual sin is criminal, and holding an individual accountable to the justice system can protect others and offer him or her an opportunity to receive help. We pray this book will help parents and therapists bring the power of God's Word and Biblical values to prevention efforts and the healing process.

If your loved one has been sexually abused it is important to consider first, the present and future safety of your child or teen. Preventing contact with the offender should begin immediately to cease further harm and potential physical and emotional consequences. This point is crucial for both the child and caregiver to understand. Secondly, a plan to help your child can begin with an assessment at your local Child Advocacy Center. These centers specialize in obtaining the necessary evidence for the legal process in a manner that is especially sensitive to abused children and their families while initiating any needed medical care, counseling services or other social supports. If no Child Advocacy Center is available in your area, a professional with training in child trauma, such as a pediatrician, psychiatrist or licensed counselor can help determine what interventions are appropriate.

Blessings and wisdom to you,

M.Ojinga & Dionne Harrison MD

About the Authors

Dionne Dillon Harrison MD is a board certified psychiatrist who completed her psychiatric residency at Duke University with additional training time spent in family therapy and working with children who have experienced abuse and neglect. She has completed various studies in Biblical counseling. She currently helps children, adolescents, and adults in private practice alongside her husband and mentor, M. Ojinga Harrison MD who is also a psychiatrist. Dr. M. Ojinga Harrison obtained his MD from University of TN at Memphis College of Medicine and completed a combined residency in internal medicine and psychiatry at Duke University. He also completed a research fellowship at the Center for Spirituality, Theology and Health. The couple is committed to a view of behavioral health and mental illness that acknowledges the impact of the fall on our humanity and our physical bodies. The Harrisons have also engaged in various training in Biblical counseling focused on compassionately and rightly dealing with the sufferings of this life. They are blessed with 4 children.

About the Illustrator

Leah Nicole Ponds was born in Youngstown, OH, but is a southern girl at heart. Raised in Charlotte, NC, Leah received her BFA with a concentration in Illustration from East Carolina University. She met her true love, Jesus Christ, in 2004. Since then, He has given her an abundant life full of peace, friendships, and opportunities to travel the world on short-term mission trips.

About the Co-Editor

Kiu Eubanks is a licensed psychologist who obtained her PhD in psychology from NY University and her EdM in Adolescent Risk and Prevention from Harvard University. She completed her clinical internship at Duke University and specializes in assessment and interventions for women and girls who have experienced trauma. Her approach to recovery blends trauma focused CBT with inspiration, insight, and faith. She is the lead clinician and executive director of Guided Pathways Psychological Services in Raleigh, NC.

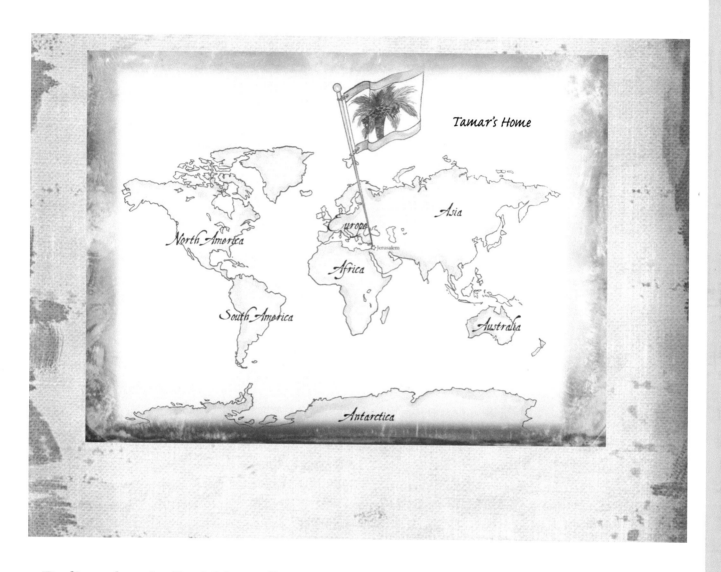

Dedicated to God's children all over the world and patients, friends and family who have shared their stories of hope and victory over sexual abuse.

May Jesus be glorified and His Word exalted!

A Letter From Tamar

Finding Victory Over Sexual Abuse and Preventing
the Cycle in Your Family

Adapted from 2 Samuel 13 by M. Ojinga & Dionne Harrison MD
Illustrated by Leah Ponds
Co-Edited by Kiu Eubanks PhD

Online Discussion Guide Available at www.ALetterFromTamar.com

This book is intended to be read to a child with the direct guidance of a parent, teacher or counselor for the purpose of preventing childhood sexual abuse and aiding in the healing process for abused children and their families. It may be harmful for a child to read this book without adequate adult supervision and explanation . This book is only part of the care plan for abused children. We strongly recommend that parents should seek professional evaluation and treatment for a child who has been abused and should not attempt to use this book as a substitute. A licensed counseling professional will determine what interventions are appropriate for a child who has been abused and whether s/he is emotionally stable enough to engage in trauma focused therapy.

Hello friends! My name is Little Luke. I love to read!!
May I introduce you to my friend, Tamar? You can find her story
in II Samuel 11. Let's go hear what she wants to teach us !!

Note: A small icon of Little Luke cues adult readers to reference the Online Discussion Cards for suggested learning objectives. These cards are designed to meet a wide range of user needs. Users are NOT expected utilize ALL of the content. They should vary its application based on the child's developmental level and setting of use.

A long time ago, even before Jesus was born, I lived in Israel where my father was the famous King David. My mother, Maacah, had two children—me and my brother, Absalom. The Bible calls me "the beautiful sister of Absalom." I even wore a coat of many colors that showed others I was special and had not been married. I also had a half brother named Amnon. He did not live with our family.

One day my half brother Amnon was sick. He asked Father to send me to his house to make a meal for him. I felt so special and happy when Father asked me to help my brother. I liked to cook and was very good at making bread and seasoning meat.

I went to Amnon's house quickly and began measuring everything I needed to make the food for him. Amnon watched me as I made the flour, oil and water into cakes and placed them in a baking pan.

When the food was ready, Amnon refused to eat. He became angry and told everyone to leave his room. What was wrong? What had they done? I hoped that I had not made him angry.

But he did not send me away. Whew!! He was not mad at me. He asked me to come into his bedroom and feed him.

I looked in his eyes and felt something was wrong. "Come lie in bed with me, my sister." He wanted to touch me in a way that a brother should not touch his sister.

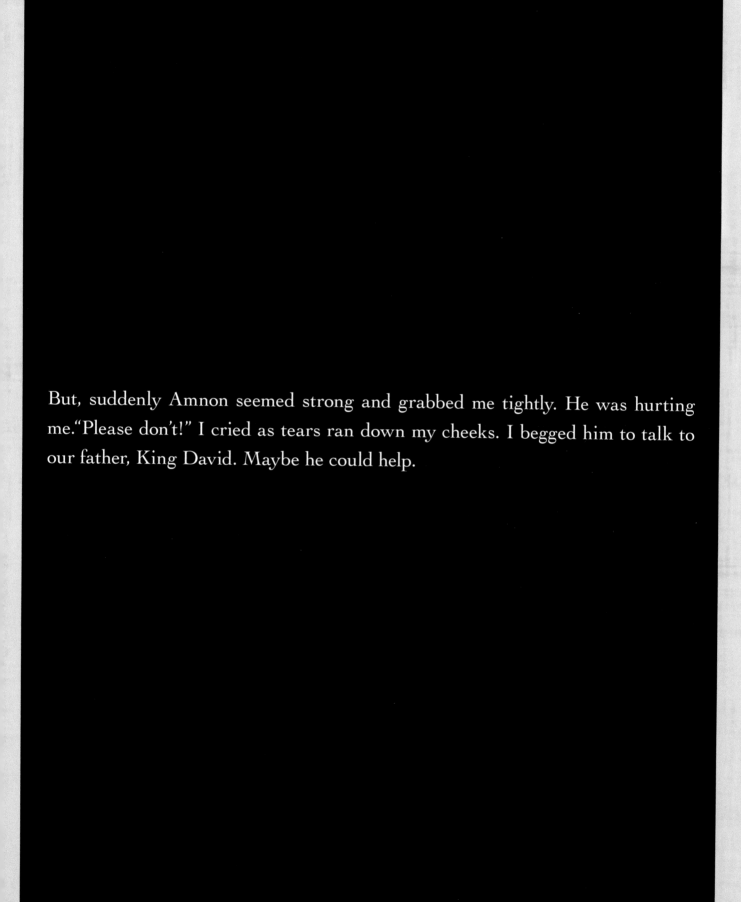

But, suddenly Amnon seemed strong and grabbed me tightly. He was hurting me."Please don't!" I cried as tears ran down my cheeks. I begged him to talk to our father, King David. Maybe he could help.

But Amnon did not listen to my voice. He kept hurting me. He was much stronger than me. He touched me in a way a brother should not touch his sister. I had so many thoughts. . .

Finally, he stopped hurting me. "Get up and get out," he yelled at me.

Then, Amnon called for his servant. "Put this stranger out. Get her away from me." He acted like I had done something wrong. The servant put me out and locked the door.

Never had I felt so sad and so very angry at the same time. I put ashes in my hair. I even tore my special royal robe of many colors. I did not have words to express what had happened to me.

As I walked away from Amnon's house, I was not sure what to do next. I soon saw my favorite brother, Absalom. Somehow he knew something was wrong. He asked if Amnon had hurt me. I was afraid to tell him at first. But then I felt strong and told him what happened. I began to feel better. I was safe with Absalom.

But Absalom, my trusted brother, whom I loved so much, told me to be quiet. Can you imagine that? I was surprised he did not want me to tell the truth. He told me not to tell anyone about how Amnon had touched me. I did not understand why he did not want anyone to know.

Truth is special to God. The truth is powerful and can protect us, even if we feel weak. God made me and YOU AMAZING! He made me brave and strong enough tell the truth.

Absalom took me to his house and protected me. My evil brother Amnon never touched me the wrong way again. What he did to me is called sexual abuse or rape. I was so glad my good brother Absalom kept Amnon from hurting me again. But, even though he protected me, he told me to be quiet and not tell anyone else. I did need to talk to others. I needed help to understand what happened to me.

I lived long ago. You are blessed to live in a time when many people can protect you and help you understand what has happened when someone has touched you the wrong way. A counselor, doctor, family, friends or pastor may all be there to help you.

In the Bible the branches of palm trees are a sign of victory. Branches of the palm tree were carried at celebrations, like when Jesus came to Jerusalem. Do you know what my name Tamar means? Palm Tree!! Palm trees grow beautiful and strong in the rough conditions of the desert. Jesus can help you do AMAZING things even when life is hard.

Like me and the palm tree God made YOU beautiful, strong and AMAZING. You are like the branch of a palm tree—a banner of victory. You will win. If you are being touched the wrong way--TELL SOMEONE. Don't be quiet until someone helps you make this person stop. Remember my story and what my name means. God loves you and so do I.

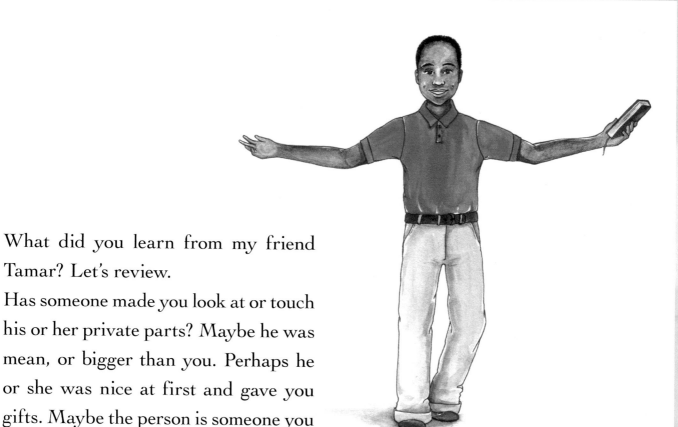

What did you learn from my friend Tamar? Let's review.

Has someone made you look at or touch his or her private parts? Maybe he was mean, or bigger than you. Perhaps he or she was nice at first and gave you gifts. Maybe the person is someone you trusted like a teacher, coach, babysitter or family member. Remember, sexual abuse can happen to ANY boy or girl. Tamar's father was a powerful and rich king. If someone has touched you the wrong way, it is NEVER YOUR FAULT.

The 3 important things to do if this happens are

1) Say "STOP" or "NO" !

2) Get to a safe place away from this person ! (if the person touching you the wrong way lives with you or is a neighbor—a trusted adult can help protect you and help you feel safe in your home again)

3) Then TELL SOMEONE THE TRUTH and don't stop until you get help !

Dear Family and Friends,

If a minor tells you they are being abused take the following steps:

1) Be calm and do not overreact. If an adult reacts negatively or with great emotion, the child may change their story or withdraw. Listen patiently.

2) Provide a safe environment for the child. Ensure the accused abuser does not have access to the child. If that person lives with the child, they should be asked to leave.

3) Report the Abuse. Contact your local child protective agency or call the police. Most states mandate individuals to report suspected abuse of a minor. Call The National Child Abuse Hotline for 24h anonymous help 1-800-4-A-CHILD.

4) Recommend/Obtain professional help. A Child Advocacy Center or pediatrician is a good place to start so that any needed clinical help will be obtained.

5) Be Courageous. The only evidence you may have is the child's word and your suspicion. Err on the side of reporting if you are unsure. The future welfare of this vulnerable child may depend on your action.

With love,
Tamar

If Abuse has Happened. . . .
The following text addresses the particular challenges for families after abuse.

*Note: Children who <u>have not</u> been abused may benefit from reading this section to learn about family mistakes, anger, justice, forgiveness, suffering and how God can help us through hard times in life. Pages 35, 36, and 37 may be less relevant to these readers.

Sometimes families and grown-ups make mistakes. My father made a big mistake. When he was told how Amnon hurt me, he did nothing. My father did not know Amnon's evil plan, but I wanted my father to say he was sorry for sending me to visit the person who hurt me. Absalom made a mistake too. He told me to keep what happened to me a secret, but I really needed to talk to someone.

Absalom needed help because he was so mad about what Amnon did to me. He did not seek JUSTICE the right way. Justice is the idea that those who do the right thing should be protected and those who do wrong must pay a penalty, like going to jail or having something valuable taken away from them. Sometimes justice requires people who have done wrong to get help so they can stop hurting others. My brother did not control his anger. Absalom's anger became so strong that he killed Amnon and fought our father.

I have learned to forgive my family for the mistakes they made. Do you know what it means to FORGIVE? When you forgive you can say, "I know what he did was wrong, but I don't want to stay angry or keep thinking about what hurt me. " Sometimes a person will say "I'm sorry for what I did to you" and will not do that thing again. In time, God can help you forgive those who have hurt you, or touched you the wrong way, even if they never say "I'm sorry. What I did was wrong."

To forgive does not mean that you forget or hide the truth. It is important that the police and maybe a court judge know if someone has touched you the wrong way so this person cannot hurt you or others again. When you forgive, it does not mean you have to be around a person who is not safe. To forgive means trusting God and the law to punish those who have hurt you.

Sometimes you may ask, "Why did God let this happen to me?" This is a hard question to answer. God is not pleased with those who hurt others. Because Adam and Eve disobeyed God in the Garden of Eden, we live in a world where all men, women, boys and girls sin. Sin is doing things that displease God, like lying, hurting others, or stealing. In this sinful world, bad things happen to everyone. Have you heard of the Hebrew boys? What a story they have! Read Daniel, chapters 1 and 3.

Shadrach, Meshach and Abednego lived during a time of war. They were taken from their families!! Their names were changed. They became servants in the palace of King Nebuchadnezzar who had captured their country. These 3 boys were of the children of Israel, God's special people. Why would God allow this to happen them? God turned their hurt into a stage for his power.

These 3 boys could have stayed angry at God for letting this happen. But instead, they became strong and trusted God to help them with their problems. God is with you like He was with these boys. He will help you. Trust Him and those He has placed to help you. You will win like these Hebrew boys. God's power will make you stronger than you can ever imagine.

It was not your fault that you were touched in a way that hurt you. Because God loves us , He gave us Christ and His power to help us to win and not lose to the pain that is a normal part of this world.

My body had many confusing feelings after I was hurt by Amnon. Girls and boys may have thoughts that they don't want to have. I was not sure I could control my body. Sometimes I had scary thoughts and bad dreams. Sometimes it was hard to pay attention to important things. There were times that my favorite food was not tasty and I did not want to play with friends.

Reading a book like this, talking about what happened and sometimes taking medicine to help you sleep or not worry so much can make things better. Like me and the palm tree God made YOU beautiful, strong and AMAZING. You are like the branch of a palm tree—a banner of victory. You will win. Remember my story and what my name means. When you are ready, you can share what happened to you with your family and counselor. God loves you and so do I.

Appendix

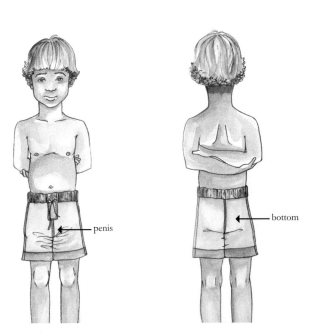

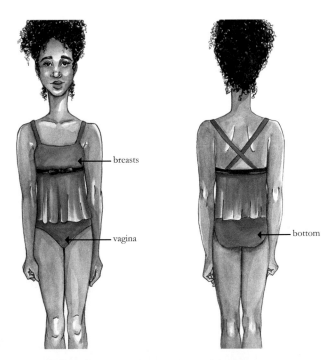

A boy's swimming trunks cover his private parts

A girl's bathing suit covers her private parts

How God Made Me: God's Purpose for My Body

God has made little boys and girls who will grow into men and women. He has created us with private parts that are important to us for many reasons. Our private parts eliminate waste from our bodies. God also has a plan that boys and girls will grow into men and women who love each other and marry. The private parts of a married man and woman are important in having children. Touching another person's private body is wrong because it can hurt boys and girls and is not how God wants our private parts to be used.

Acknowledgments

We are so grateful to the families we counsel and many people (in addition to our wonderful illustrator Leah Ponds and co-Editor Dr. Kiu Eubanks PhD) who helped us press on to complete this project. Your review and critiques have been invaluable to the creation of A Letter from Tamar. Special thanks to Ms. Evelyn Gayton and her undying love for children; Dr. Eric Greaux, Sr. PhD for his theological critique; Dr. Patrick L. Wooden Sr. and First Lady Pamela Wooden of The Upper Room COGIC for their pastoral leadership and commitment to sound Biblical doctrine; Dr. Cherry Chevy MD for her review and mentorship as a child psychiatrist; Dr. Gabriel Rogers PhD and Stephanie Rogers of Kingdom Christian Church for their review and enthusiasm for Christian counseling; Ms. Bria Arline for her awesome editoral skills; Mrs. Cora Strickland LPC of Solutions Community Support Agency for her review and experience with children and families; Mrs. LeKenna Hicks for her review and ideas for parent users; Ms. Renee Pinkney for inspiring our website design; and Ms. Vickie Adams for her publicity support and reviews. We are forever indebted to our parents, Mr. Leonard R. Harrison, Dr. Alferdteen Harrison PhD, Dr. Alva Dillon Jr. MD and Mrs. Dianne Dillon for their many gifts to us especially their love for Christ and us as their children. Finally, as parents, we thank our children-Alferdteen, Abigail, Apollos and Amara for their unique contribution and response to our first children's book. All praise is due to Jesus Christ our Savior and King!

M. Ojinga & Dionne Harrison

Printed in the United States
by Baker & Taylor Publisher Services